Although it gives little idea of the actual sound, the following is the specification of the organ completed in 1724 by the firm of Renatus Harris for St. Dionis Backchurch, Fenchurch Street, London. This church, which was rebuilt after the Great Fire of 1666 from the designs of Sir Christopher Wren, was demolished in 1879. John Bennett was organist from 1752 until 1784, having succeeded Charles Burney.

Great (*GG to D*)
Open Diapason 8
Stopped Diapason 8
Principal 4
Twelfth $2\frac{2}{3}$ Fifteenth 2 (one stop)
Tierce $1\frac{3}{5}$
Larigot $1\frac{1}{3}$
Sesquialtera (4 ranks)
Cornet (from middle C up) (5 ranks)
Trumpet 8
French Horn (from Tenor D up) 8
Clarion 4
Cremona 8 (from Choir)

Swell (*from fiddle G*)
Open Diapason 8
Stopped Diapason 8
Cornet (4 ranks)
Trumpet 8
Clarion 4
Cremona 8
Vox Humana 8

Choir
Open Diapason 8
Stopped Diapason 8
Principal 4
Flute 4
Bassoon
Cremona 8
Clarion 4 (from Great)
Vox Humana 8

Book 3
Contents

PREFACE

In choice of stops the aim should be clarity, particularly in the louder pieces. Although changes of manual are sometimes indicated, all the pieces in this book can be played effectively on a one-manual organ.

In the original editions there are frequently no directions either for registration or tempo. Apart from which manual to be used [e.g. Great, Swell, Chair (sometimes Chaire or Chayre) i.e. the equivalent of the German *Rückpositiv*—the *positiv* organ at the back of the player], the usual directions are Trumpet, Cornet, Vox Humana, Flute, Diapasons, Eccho, Soft Organ, Loud, and Full Organ—the latter being the full organ of the composer's time.

Full Organ is probably best realised by the following:

Gt. light Diapasons 8.4. (2⅔.) 2. Mixture.

or Gt. light Diapasons 8.4. (2.) coupled to Sw. Diapasons 8.4.2. Mixture. (box open)

If harsh or strident, the Mixture should not be used in either case.

Following are suggestions for registration with equivalents:

Gt. light Diapasons 8.4. (2.)=Small Open Diapason (or Flute) 8. Principal 4. (Fifteenth 2.)

Gt. light 8.4.2.=Flutes 8.4. Fifteenth 2.

Gt. light 8.2.=Small Open Diapason (or Flute) 8. Fifteenth 2.

Light 8.4.= Gt. Flute (or Dulciana) 8. Flute 4. [or Ch. Flutes 8.4.]

In most cases Stopped Diapason 8. is probably better than Flute 8. The large Open Diapason 8. should *not* be used.

Cornet Voluntaries. If there is no Cornet, the following alternatives are suggested:

$\begin{cases} \text{R.H. Gt. light 8.4.2. (or 8.2.)} \\ \text{L.H. Sw. 8.4. (2.) [Sw. to Gt. ?]} \end{cases}$

or $\begin{cases} \text{R.H. Sw. Oboe 8. [or 8 ft. stop(s)]. Fifteenth 2. (Mixture.)} \\ \text{L.H. Ch. 8.4. (2.) [or Gt. soft 8 (4.)]} \end{cases}$

or Gt. (or Sw. or Ch.) 8.4.2. both hands

In the latter case and if the organ is a one-manual, for the echo or dialogue effects, a stop (2 ft. ?) could be withdrawn or the passage phrased differently e.g. *staccato*.

Trumpet Voluntaries. The Tuba should *not* be used. If there is no Trumpet, the following alternatives are suggested:

$\begin{cases} \text{R.H. Gt. Diapason(s) 8. (4.)} \\ \text{L.H. Sw. 8.4. (2.) [Sw. to Gt. ?]} \end{cases}$

or Gt. light Diapason(s) 8.4. (2.) both hands

In the latter case and if the organ is a one-manual, the echo or dialogue effects could be played as suggested in the Cornet Voluntaries.

Stops with the same names do not always produce the same effect on different organs. Players should use other registrations if those suggested are not effective or suitable on any particular instrument.

The directions for registration which are enclosed in brackets may be used or not at the player's discretion.

The tempo indications are the composer's except those enclosed in brackets which are the editor's.

C.H.T.

OLD ENGLISH ORGAN MUSIC

Edited by C. H. TREVOR

Book III

GAVOTTE

(Organ solo from a Concerto)

Gt. light 8. 4.
Sw. 8. 4. (2.)
Sw. to Gt.

Matthew Camidge (1758-1844)

VOLUNTARY IN D MINOR

Not fast { Gt. light Diapasons 8. 4. (2.)
{ Sw. 8. 4. 2. box open
Moderato { Gt. light Diapasons 8. 4. (2.)
{ Sw. 8. 4. 2. (Mixture.) box closed
{ Sw. to Gt.

William Boyce (1710-1779)

The composer's registration: Full Organ (see preface)

The suggested changes of manual are the composer's.

The *poco a poco cresc.* should be made by gradually opening the swell box. The new "swelling organ", as it was called, was introduced in 1712 by Abraham Jordan at the church of St. Magnus the Martyr, London Bridge. In his "Present state of music in France and Italy", Burney complains of finding no swell organs in 1770. Three stops were placed in a swell-box in the organ of St. Michael's Church, Hamburg, but with so little effect that Burney, who heard the organ in 1762, says that if he had not been told there was a swell he would not have noticed it.

SICILIANO
(from a voluntary)

Ch. Flutes 8. 4.
(or Sw. Diapason 8.)

John Alcock junr. (1740-1791)

ALLEGRO
(Organo Solo from a Concerto)

Gt. light Diapasons 8. 4. (2.)
[or Gt. Flutes 8. 4. Fifteenth 2.]

Thomas Arne (1710-1778)

Old English Organ Music for Manuals (Vol. III)

FLUTE PIECE

light Flute (s) 8. (4.)

William Hine (1687-1730)

VOLUNTARY IN A MINOR

John James (died 1745)

ADAGIO
(from a voluntary)

Sw. Diapason 8.
(or Ch. Flutes 8. 4.)

John Bennett (1735-1784)

DIAPASON MOVEMENT
(from a voluntary)

Maurice Greene (1695-1755)

TRUMPET VOLUNTARY

Thomas Sanders Dupuis (1733-1796)

★See preface for alternative registrations.

Old English Organ Music for Manuals (Vol. III)

CORNET VOLUNTARY

William Walond (1725-1770)

Allegro

★See preface for alternative registrations.

Old English Organ Music for Manuals (Vol. III)

Old English Organ Music for Manuals (Vol. III)

VOLUNTARY IN F

Gt. light Diapasons 8. 4. (2.)
Sw. Diapason 8.

John Bennett (1735-1784)

The composer's registration for *Allegro:* Full Organ (see preface)

The original edition has no suggestion for changes of manual. If players prefer, the *Allegro* can be played throughout on the Gt. uncoupled or coupled to Sw.

THREE INTERLUDES

Starling Goodwin (18th century)

Processed and printed by
Halstan & Co. Ltd., Amersham, Bucks., England

OXFORD UNIVERSITY PRESS